inkblots

A CREATIVE WRITING SYLLABUS

by Pat Watson

ECS
Learning Systems
INC.

Editor: Jennifer Knoblock
Page Layout & Graphics: Kathryn Riches
Cover/Book Design: Educational Media Services

These popular series of books are available from ECS Learning Systems, Inc.

Structures for Reading, Writing, Thinking	Gr. 4-9	4 Titles
Writing Warm-Ups™	Gr. K-6 & 7-12	4 Titles
Foundations for Writing	Gr. 2-8	2 Titles
Springboards for Reading	Gr. 3-6 & 7-12	2 Titles
Booklinks to American and World History	Gr. 4-8	12 Titles
The Picture Book Companion	Gr. K-3	3 Titles
Novel Extenders	Gr. 1-6	7 Titles
Literature Guides	Gr. 7-12	17 Titles
Building Language Power	Gr. 4-9	3 Titles
Quick Thinking™	Gr. K-12	2 Titles
Thematic Units	Gr. K-8	23 Titles
Activity Books	Gr. K-12	11 Titles
EnviroLearn™	Gr. K-5	5 Titles
Home Study Collection™(Basic Skills & More)	Gr. 1-6	18 Titles
Test Preparation Guides	Gr. 2-12	41 Titles

Other Activity Books

Not More Writing?!	Gr. 9-12
Passageways	Gr. 5-9
Booklinks	Gr. 3-8
Tactics to Tackle Thinking	Gr. 6-12

To order, contact your local school supply store, or write/call for a complete catalog:

ECS Learning Systems, Inc.
P.O. Box 791437
San Antonio, Texas 78279-1437

ACKNOWLEDGMENTS

To my husband, W.T.,
for his unfailing love, support, and encouragement

I wish to thank those who have encouraged and helped me
as I have prepared this syllabus for teaching creative writing:

To my children and their families:
David and Debbie,
Ed and Kim,
Clifford and Janet

Wayland Ethridge,
my principal

Hellen Adrian

Barbara Milburn

My colleagues at Muleshoe High School
for their encouragement as I have developed this program

My students in the creative writing classroom,
for their response to the course and
for their contributions to the syllabus

TABLE OF CONTENTS

PREFACE

The objective of a creative writing course is to guide students as they learn to express themselves in a variety of literary genres. Creative writing requires that students be able to hear, to feel, to touch, to see, and to think and wonder. The exercises in this book are designed to challenge students to channel their thoughts, feelings, and observations into writing.

This book is divided into four sections: Getting Started, Unit Plans, Student Handouts, and Student Work. The Getting Started section includes activities and suggestions for introducing creative writing to the students. Hopefully, these activities will help the students open up and encourage them to have fun with writing. The Unit Plans section is a suggested syllabus for the creative writing course. Each unit states an objective, focus activity, process for teaching, and assignment. In addition, some lessons include an extension activity for students who wish to continue on their own. The Student Handout section includes handouts referenced in the various lessons. The Student Work section includes examples of the various genres, generated by creative writing students.

The Unit Plans have been organized so that the lessons build on one another. Early lessons provide experience in different writing styles. These early lessons also develop student awareness and skill in areas such as imagery, characterization, and point of view. The final lessons require the students to "put it all together;" to write short stories and poetry which include all the elements they've studied.

The teacher's participation is a vital part of any creative writing program. If the teacher enthusiastically shares his/her ideas and own writing with the students, they will recognize that learning and growing are never-ending processes. Flexibility is also integral to a creative writing program. Neither the teacher nor the students should feel limited by any of the assignments.

I began to develop this program five years ago, when we established a creative writing program at Muleshoe High School, Texas. I hope this program will be as fun and successful for other schools as it has been for us.

GETTING STARTED

WARMING UP

The first week in a creative writing class is vitally important. The teacher must establish rapport with the students, and the students must begin to feel comfortable with one another. Include some assignments that are just for fun as well as some that can be used constructively in future assignments. This is a good time to have students begin their journals. It is also beneficial to discuss with the students what they want to achieve in a creative writing course.

Consider the following ideas for the first week.

- Wacky wordies (available in several books)
- Rebus riddles (also available in several books)
- Rhyming Riddles (see Student Handout 1, p. 54)
- Palindromes
- Newspaper headlines—Take an unusual headline and write it on the board. Have students write an article they think would go with this headline. Read some of the students' articles aloud. Then read the original article.
- Read short selections that use strong visual imagery. Discuss how the writer paints a word picture. Have students write a brief description of something they have recently seen, heard, or tasted.
- Have students brainstorm and list several "tales." Have students work with partners to develop a descriptive paragraph about one of the tales.
- Have each student choose a person in the room (without identifying the person) and write a description of him/her. Read these aloud and have students guess who is being described.
- Have each student choose an object in the room and write a description. Read these aloud and have students guess the object.
- Create puns.
- Create sentences using alliteration.
- Using examples from "Toward More Picturesque Speech" in the *Reader's Digest,* have students create some originals.
- Pair each student with a partner. Have partners sit back to back. Have each one select a line drawing and describe this figure to his/her partner, who is to draw what is being described.
- Blindfold students. Give each one an unusual object. After the student has manually examined the object, take the object and remove the blindfold. Have the student write a description of the object.

JOURNAL IDEAS

Student journals are assets in a creative writing class. By recording thoughts, students can recapture a scene, an idea, a mood, or an event. The journal is also a useful device for recording various lists, observations, mental photographs, and catchy expressions or words. As their journals expand, students generate many ideas for writing projects. Journals are personal, and students should feel free to record their feelings. The teacher should practice confidentiality. In fact, for this type of journal, a teacher may choose not to read it at all unless a student asks for help or wants someone to read what has been written. Ideas for journal prompts and list ideas follow.

I REMEMBER LISTS

the first time...
the last time...
a trip...
an illness...
a frightening experience...
first day at school...
an embarrassing incident...
a unique conversation...
odd characters I have known...
my first experience with death...
when I encountered prejudice...
when I wanted to run away...
my first date (kiss, boyfriend, girlfriend, etc.)...
a total breakdown of communication...
dreams...
happy times in my past...
sad times in my past...

MENTAL SNAPSHOTS

noun + strong verb (dishes clattering, sirens shrieking)
a child (crying, playing)
parents (pleased, angry, perturbed, frightened)
teacher (first grade, etc.)
sights (describe as for a blind person)
expressions
mannerisms
unusual clothing

VARIOUS LISTS

likes (food, pets, etc.)
dislikes (habits, food, chores)
objects (in a room, pocket, purse)
favorites (people, places, possessions, movies, TV shows, nursery rhymes, fairy tales)
words or phrases (unique, pleasant, unpleasant, unknown)
past (memories, friends, trips)
future (dreams, plans)
odd characters
large things
small things
today (what I've seen, where I've been)
difficult tasks
unfinished things
sounds (pleasant and unpleasant)

PROMPTS

I respect people who…
People who are sarcastic make me…
When a friend shares a problem with me, I…
I wish I could be more…
Sometimes I am afraid of…
Prejudice makes me…
If I could have one wish, I would choose…
I dislike people who…
If I were in charge of the world, I would…
My worst fault is…
I most admire…because…
I am a good friend because…
My greatest asset is…
The political upheaval in the world makes me…
The threat of nuclear war makes me…
I believe…
If I could change one thing about me, it would be…
If I were stranded on an island, I would want…
In ten years, I hope…
Sometimes my parents…

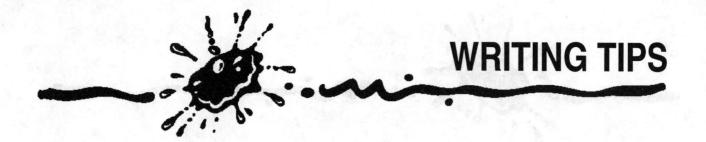

WRITING TIPS

The following suggestions help strengthen student writing. These suggestions might serve as a checklist to help keep the class focused or to polish any piece of writing.

I.   Experiment with a variety of sentence beginnings.

    A.   Subject followed by adjective

    B.   Adverb

    C.   Prepositional phrase

    D.   Subordinate adverbial clause

    E.   Adjective

    F.   Present participle

    G.   Past participle

    H.   Infinitive

    I.   Absolute phrase

    J.   Coordinating conjunction

II. Remember the seven C's of composition.

    A.   Clarity

    B.   Coherence

    C.   Completeness

    D.   Conciseness

    E.   Concreteness

    F.   Continuity

    G.   Correctness

 ©ECS Learning Systems, Inc., San Antonio, Texas

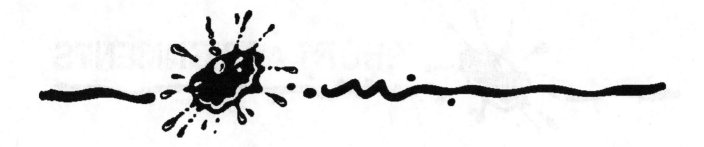

III. Rely on several methods for revision.

    A.   Student/teacher conferences

    B.   Teacher-directed revision (via written comments on returned paper)

    C.   Group questions

    D.   Peer evaluation

    E.   Tutorial sessions

IV. Practice to improve proofreading skills.

    A.   Read slowly

    B.   Examine each line

    C.   Be aware of usual errors

    D.   Cross out errors neatly

    E.   Check dictionary

SHORT ASSIGNMENTS

CREATIVE WRITING SHORT ASSIGNMENTS

These assignments can be used at any time during the course. Each assignment should take only one day.

Assignment 1:

1. Write a ten-word sentence in which "today" is the first word.
2. Write a ten-word sentence in which "today" is the second word.
3. Write a ten-word sentence in which "today" is the third word.
4. Write a ten-word sentence in which "today" is the fourth word.
5. Write a ten-word sentence in which "today" is the fifth word.
6. Write a ten-word sentence in which "today" is the sixth word.
7. Write a ten-word sentence in which "today" is the seventh word.
8. Write a ten-word sentence in which "today" is the eighth word.
9. Write a ten-word sentence in which "today" is the ninth word.
10. Write a ten-word sentence in which "today" is the tenth word.

Assignment 2:

Write a letter to the editor of the local paper or to the school principal in which you express an opinion about an issue which concerns you.

Assignment 3:

Write a letter in which you reveal an experience where you...

felt you had to lie
discovered a hidden strength
became lost
felt overwhelmed by superstition
encountered prejudice
experienced a total breakdown in communication

Assignment 4:

Reveal someone's personality by describing his/her car, pocket contents, purse contents, clothes closet, desk drawer, locker, or anything else that might reveal the person's public profile as well as his/her inner self.

©ECS Learning Systems, Inc., San Antonio, Texas

Assignment 5:

Construct an imaginary dialogue between contrasting individuals. Consider sports figures, political opponents, parent/child, student/teacher—any two individuals who, for the moment at least, have definitely contrasting views. In your dialogue, find ways for the characters to reveal more about themselves than they intended to reveal.

Assignment 6:

Write a detailed entry in your journal today. Consider these suggestions:

If I could select one keepsake from today, what would it be and why would I choose it?

If I could forget one specific thing from today, what would it be and why would I like to forget it?

If I were to select a color that would describe today, what would it be and why?

As I consider the people I have encountered today, what would I like to say to one of them that I did not say?

Assignment 7:

Write a first-person narrative paragraph in which the speaker demonstrates sarcasm.

Assignment 8:

Write a descriptive paragraph about the most obstinate person you have ever known. Expand your ideas by illustrative anecdotes.

Assignment 9:

Design a greeting card. Write a message that expresses emotion about a particular situation or occasion.

To be creative is to have the power to create, to invest, to produce, to be imaginative, to be constructive, to be purposeful, and to develop something useful or worthwhile.

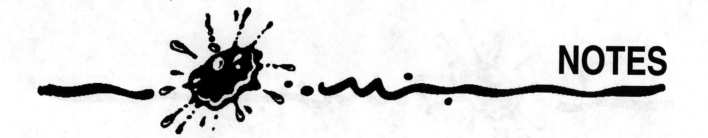

NOTES

UNIT PLANS

DESCRIPTIVE WRITING

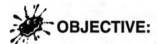

OBJECTIVE:

To demonstrate an understanding of descriptive writing style by writing a paragraph that appeals to the five senses

FOCUS ACTIVITY:

Display a picture from a magazine. The picture should include many details. Have students verbally describe what they see in the picture.

PROCESS:

Distribute Student Handout 2 (p. 56), "Types of Writing." Discuss descriptive writing. Have several pictures, involving a variety of subjects, available for the students to view.

©ECS Learning Systems, Inc., San Antonio, Texas

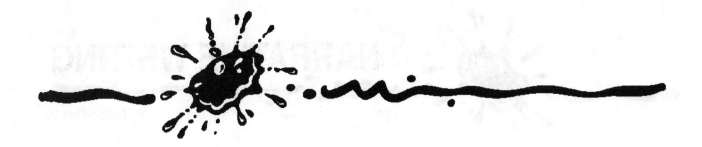

 ASSIGNMENT:

Each student chooses a picture and writes random ideas about what is in the picture. After pre-writing, the student writes a descriptive paragraph that includes sensory detail. The student's writing should appeal to all the senses.

EXTENSION:

Students develop a written "snapshot" of a place they have recently visited or an unusual object they have recently seen.

OBJECTIVE:

To write a selection which demonstrates an understanding of narrative writing style

FOCUS ACTIVITY:

Display a picture of a person who seems to be in a pensive or reflective mood. Discuss how the person might be feeling and what experience might have led to this mood.

PROCESS:

Discuss narrative writing. Refer students to Student Handout 2 (p. 56), "Types of Writing." Have several pictures of people available. Select pictures with people engaged in a variety of activities or with people showing an obvious mood or attitude (happiness, disgust, etc.).

©ECS Learning Systems, Inc., San Antonio, Texas

ASSIGNMENT:

Students choose and complete one of the following assignments.

1.   Each student chooses a picture and writes a narrative about the person, including ideas such as name, age, occupation, attitude about life, and thoughts on the occasion pictured. If the student's picture shows a person involved in an activity, (s)he could relate the events that preceded the activity as well as the person's feelings about the activity. If the person in the picture displays a particular emotion or attitude, the student could relate something that happened to cause the emotion, and three events that might occur from that point on.

2.   Students read Student Handout 3 (p. 57), "Narrative Writing (Personal Experience)." Each student completes the assignment which follows the excerpt. For an example of narrative writing, refer to the Student Work section, p. 86.

EXTENSION:

Students can select an entry from their journals and rewrite it as a narrative.

EXPOSITORY WRITING

LESSON 3

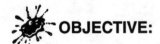 **OBJECTIVE:**

To demonstrate an understanding of expository writing style by writing step-by-step instructions to a particular place

FOCUS ACTIVITY:

Have an object hidden in the classroom. Give clues as to its hiding place until someone finds it.

PROCESS:

Discuss types of expository writing such as directions, explanations, rationales, etc. Refer students to Student Handout 2 (p. 56), "Types of Writing." Explain that the clues given for a hiding place are information needed for the seeker to find the hidden object.

©ECS Learning Systems, Inc., San Antonio, Texas

 ASSIGNMENT:

Each student imagines that (s)he owns something valuable and has selected a hiding place for the treasure. The student writes a set of directions for getting to the hiding place from a selected starting point.

EXTENSION:

The variations for expository writing are endless, ranging from step-by-step instructions for building something to an explanation of the meaning of life!

PERSUASIVE WRITING

 **OBJECTIVE:**

To write a selection which demonstrates an understanding of persuasive writing techniques

FOCUS ACTIVITY:

Display ads from a magazine or newspaper; be sure they use several persuasive words (biggest, best, etc.). Discuss how these ads are designed to persuade the reader to buy a certain product.

PROCESS:

Discuss persuasive writing. Refer to Student Handout 2 (p. 56), "Types of Writing." This is a good time to identify hyperbole*. Have available newspaper ads and editorials. Discuss different approaches used to persuade.

*an intentional exaggeration used as a figure of speech and not intended to be taken literally

©ECS Learning Systems, Inc., San Antonio, Texas

ASSIGNMENT:

Students choose and complete one of the following assignments.

1.   The student chooses an issue of concern and writes a newspaper editorial or letter to the editor about the issue.

2.   Each student writes a letter to persuade a friend of a different opinion about an important teenage issue (drugs, abortion, suicide, sex, etc.)

3.   Students write a dialogue to persuade their parents to let them attend a rock concert. They should consider such issues as adverse publicity, distance to the concert, age of student, etc.

ADVERTISING

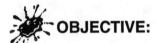

OBJECTIVE:

To develop an idea for a new product
To produce an advertising campaign for the new product

FOCUS ACTIVITY:

Have a variety of advertising brochures available. Discuss slogans, artwork, pictures, and other eye-catching details.

PROCESS:

Continue by discussing the types of advertising that appeal to today's teenagers. Include TV commercials and printed advertising. Discuss the impact of various types of advertising, both positive and negative. Analyze subtle and obvious techniques used to secure the reader's or viewer's attention.

©ECS Learning Systems, Inc., San Antonio, Texas

ASSIGNMENT:

Students work in groups of two or three. Each group chooses a product that the students wish to invent or a remedy they wish to develop. The group must then:

1. select a name for the product

2. establish a rationale

3. design an advertising campaign which includes slogans, artwork, dialogue for TV commercials, or other ideas.

For an example of advertising campaigns, refer to the Student Work section, p. 87.

EXTENSION:

Students present their advertising campaigns to the class. A variety of formats can be used, including a video presentation, a skit, handouts or flyers, or models of the product with accompanying data. Before the presentation, the group should state the rationale, targeted audience, and most effective type of campaign for the product or remedy.

Grade students on creativity (play on words, analogies, etc.), originality, and overall effectiveness.

VISUAL IMAGERY

OBJECTIVE:

To demonstrate an understanding of effective use of imagery

FOCUS ACTIVITY:

Before class begins, write a word such as "phonophobia" (fear of speaking out loud) on the board. Discuss various phobias and share experiences involving fear.

PROCESS:

Discuss how vibrant imagery enhances writing. Read students a suspenseful scene from a short story or novel. Have students point out particular images that helped them visualize the scene or made them feel they were part of the action.

 ASSIGNMENT:

Each student writes a descriptive scene involving fear and suspense. This can be based on a real or imaginary experience. The scene must include evocative imagery, so the reader or listener will sense the fear the writer experienced.

Completed papers may be read orally on a volunteer basis.

EXTENSION:

Students research various phobias. They select one of these phobias and write a scene involving that fear. Students might also take root words and create their own phobias, such as biophobia (fear of life).

INTERPRETIVE WRITING

 **OBJECTIVE:**

To listen to a variety of musical selections
To write a descriptive paragraph which expresses the mood created by the music

FOCUS ACTIVITY:

Play a selection of classical music as students enter the classroom. Discuss the mood the selection creates.

PROCESS:

Have available a variety of musical selections to play in the classroom. Include classical and popular classics as well as music that students currently enjoy. Play several of these and have the students write words or phrases that describe the mental picture the music creates. Some classical compositions that work well include "Sabre Dance," Khachaturian; "La Traviata," Verdi; "The Flight of the Bumble Bee," Rimsky-Korsakov; "Skater's Waltz," Strauss; and "Reflections on the Water," by Debussy. Themes from movies usually evoke strong images, also.

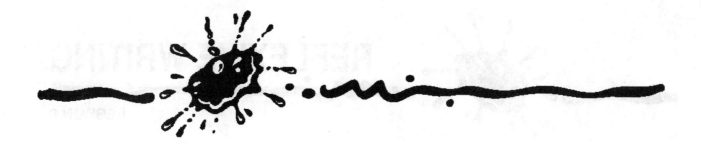

 **ASSIGNMENT:**

Each student takes images from one or two of the compositions and develops a descriptive paragraph that paints a mental picture of his/her interpretation of the music.

EXTENSION:

After all the assignments are complete, allow students to bring recordings of their favorite music; listen to several of these and discuss the students' interpretations. Be sure to offer your interpretation, also!

REFLEXIVE WRITING

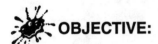

OBJECTIVE:

To revise a reflexive, non-structured piece of writing into a structured, coherent passage

FOCUS ACTIVITY:

Have students write non-stop for five minutes (whatever comes to mind). Discuss student re-action and ask for volunteers to read what they have written. Discuss how writing can be unorganized and scattered when there is no structure or goal in mind.

PROCESS:

Have students brainstorm topic ideas, including people, places, and events. Ideas might include:

People: mysterious, humorous, friendly, noble, dedicated

Places: scary, cozy, exciting, beautiful, threatening, peaceful

Events: frightening, rewarding, embarrassing, unusual, exciting

©ECS Learning Systems, Inc., San Antonio, Texas

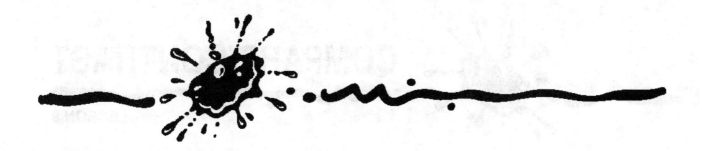

ASSIGNMENT:

Students choose a specific person, place, or event. For ten minutes, each student writes non-stop about the chosen topic. After writing, students exchange papers and make suggestions for revision. Each student then revises and rewrites the paper as a structured piece with an introduction, development, and suitable conclusion. The brainstormed ideas can be added to the students' journals for future writing assignments.

COMPARE/CONTRAST

 **OBJECTIVE:**

To demonstrate an understanding of points of comparison and/or contrast
To use transitions between ideas
To edit the work of someone else

FOCUS ACTIVITY:

On an overhead transparency or chalkboard, write a pair of contrasting words, such as war/peace. Have students brainstorm and list differences and/or similarities in the two concepts.

PROCESS:

Discuss comparison and contrast. Divide the class into groups of three or four students each. The students choose someone to record the group's ideas. Each group discusses and chooses two items the students want to compare or contrast. Students brainstorm. If comparing two items, the students list ways in which the items are the same; if contrasting, they list ways in which the items are different.

**ASSIGNMENT:**

Day 1:
Using ideas from the group's list, each student writes a statement that tells the reader what is being compared or contrasted.

Students write paragraphs, elaborating on their thesis statements. Students must write examples or explanations which reinforce each point of comparison or contrast. This section can include one or two paragraphs, depending on the amount of information the students have.

Ideas within a paragraph need to be linked with transitional words or phrases. If there is more than one paragraph, paragraphs must be joined together with a transitional expression. Each student writes a strong concluding sentence for his/her paper.

Day 2:
Students read and revise their papers. The points of comparison or contrast should be organized into a cohesive paper. The paper should contain a thesis sentence, several points of comparison or contrast, transitional words that connect the ideas, and a strong concluding sentence.

Day 3:
Students exchange papers. Students analyze the papers and record the following information.

1. State the two items that are being compared or contrasted.

2. Underline the thesis statement of the paper.

3. List the primary points of comparison or contrast.

4. List the transitional words used to connect ideas.

5. Underline the concluding sentence.

6. Circle and identify any errors in mechanics.

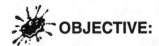

OBJECTIVE:

To meet and get to know someone (student or teacher) who is new to the school
To record information using descriptive and narrative writing skills

FOCUS ACTIVITY:

If a student who has just transferred to the school is enrolled in the class, have him/her relate impressions and feelings about the move. If not, discuss what it might be like to be a new student or teacher in a school.

PROCESS:

Discuss interviewing techniques and brainstorm communication skills (proper approach, types of questions, etc.). Have students design a questionnaire for an interview; it should include investigation of the subject's background, memories, ideas about the new school, etc.

After students have conducted the interviews, present ideas for translating the facts into a well-written composition that incorporates descriptive and narrative literary devices.

©ECS Learning Systems, Inc., San Antonio, Texas

 ASSIGNMENT:

Each student chooses one newcomer to the school or community. To avoid overlap, names should be chosen and posted. Each student makes an appointment with the person to be interviewed. The student may develop a new questionnaire or use the one developed by the class. After completing the interview, each student translates the ideas and information from the interview into a descriptive, narrative composition.

EXTENSION:

Students complete one of the following activities.

1.   Students interview an elderly person and record his/her views on some specific event in history, such as the Great Depression.

2.   Students interview someone who is involved in an unfamiliar occupation or hobby. Then they write an expository paper in which they record information about the activity.

PERSONALITY PROFILE

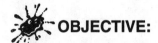 **OBJECTIVE:**

To relate selected objects to a particular personality
To compose a personality profile of an imaginary person

FOCUS ACTIVITY:

Place a suitcase on the desk. Open it and remove various items. Discuss the type of person who might own these items.

PROCESS:

Have each student pretend (s)he has picked up the wrong suitcase at the airport. Read to the students the list of items found in the suitcase (p. 41). Discuss what thoughts went through the students' minds as you read the list.

ASSIGNMENT:

Based on what is in the suitcase, each student develops a short paper that reveals the owner's character and personality.

The suitcase contents:

> a library card from UCLA
>
> a pair of 501 jeans (32" waist, 36" length)
>
> pictures of 5 different girls
>
> an advanced anatomy book
>
> a bundle of dirty laundry
>
> an extra-large Boston Marathon T-shirt
>
> a kit for waxing skis
>
> a bank deposit slip for $229.51
>
> a bill for one dozen roses
>
> a "little black book" filled with girls' phone numbers and addresses
>
> a medical dictionary
>
> a pair of Reebok jogging shoes
>
> a Bible
>
> a hospital scrub suit
>
> a gift-wrapped package tagged "To Marcy"
>
> an unpaid speeding ticket
>
> two ticket stubs from the opera
>
> an unfinished letter beginning "Dear Paula"

CHARACTERIZATION

OBJECTIVE:

To write a characterization which reveals the physical and mental qualities of a person

FOCUS ACTIVITY:

Display a picture of a person who is unknown to the students. Discuss the person's physical characteristics and have the students share ideas about what the person's facial expressions might reveal about him/her. After the students have expressed their ideas, tell them what the person is/was really like.

PROCESS:

1. Create a personalized T-shirt. Distribute Student Handout 4 (p. 58), "Personality T-shirt." Have students develop a slogan and/or design which reflects their personality. Discuss differences in personalities.

2. Choose a model for class observation. This model can be a volunteer from the class, an adult, or a child. One effective class model is a preschool child. The students observe the model for thirty minutes. During this time they should write their observations about the physical characteristics and personality of the model. Discuss observations; compile information.

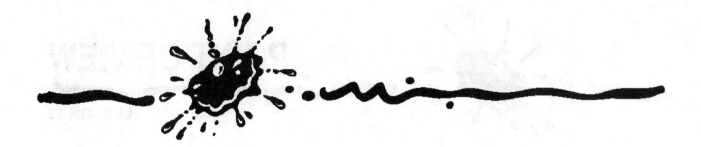

ASSIGNMENT:

Group Activity:

1. In groups of three or four, students use the information about the model and develop one paragraph about the model. For example, group one could write a physical description, group two could write a personality description, and group three could write a prediction for the model's future. Depending on the number of students in the class, another group could write an introductory paragraph and a conclusion. The class takes the group paragraphs and develops a composite characterization. The composite sketch is read aloud, and each student receives a copy. Be sure to send a copy to the person who served as the model for the characterization.

Individual Assignment:

2. Each student chooses a person who has had an impact on his/her life and writes a characterization of that person. This characterization should include the physical, mental, emotional, and spiritual qualities of the selected person. Students work on the assignment in class. This gives the instructor an opportunity to work one-on-one with each student.

For examples of characterization, refer to the Student Work section, pp. 88-90.

POINT OF VIEW

LESSON 13

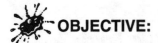 **OBJECTIVE:**

To rewrite a familiar story from a different point of view

FOCUS ACTIVITY:

Distribute Student Handout 5 (pp. 59-60), "The Three Little Pigs—Revised," and read it to the class. Discuss the change from the traditional point of view.

PROCESS:

Discuss a variety of fairy tales. Have students identify the protagonist, antagonist, and the characters from whose point of view each story is written. Discuss how each story might change if told from another character's point of view.

©ECS Learning Systems, Inc., San Antonio, Texas

 **ASSIGNMENT:**

Students complete one of the following assignments.

1. Each student rewrites a fairy tale from an opposite point of view. The protagonist and antagonist roles will be reversed, and situations will change to fit the plot. For example, "Cinderella" might be retold from the point of view of the stepmother who has been given the awesome task of raising a spoiled stepchild.

2. Students write a short piece about an incident, from their point of view (first person). Then, they write about the same incident from one of the following points of view:

    > someone else who was directly involved
    > an "innocent" bystander
    > a TV crew covering the story
    > a visitor from Mars
    > their mom or dad

EXTENSION:

Students rewrite a scene from a short story or novel to reflect a different character's point of view. For example, they could rewrite one of the scenes from *To Kill a Mockingbird* from Boo Radley's point of view.

SHORT STORY

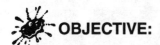 **OBJECTIVE:**

To demonstrate an understanding of elements of fiction (including point of view, characterization, and plot development) by writing a short story

FOCUS ACTIVITY:

Have students recall a favorite short story. Discuss why certain short stories appeal to the reader. Another possible focus is to discuss a short story read recently in a literature class. Discuss positive and negative points of the story and its overall interest level.

PROCESS:

1. Read and analyze a short story such as "The Necklace" by Guy DeMaupassant. Discuss the five parts of the plot development. Discuss literary devices such as point of view, foreshadowing, suspense, etc.

2. Distribute Student Handouts 7-10. Student Handout 6 (p. 61), "Short Story Assignment," is the writing assignment for this unit. Student Handout 7 (pp. 62-63), "Planning Sheet," is to help students organize their stories. Student Handout 8 (pp. 64-65), "Structure and Elements of Plot," makes a good student reference. Student Handout 9 (p. 66), "Story Starters," will help students generate story ideas.

©ECS Learning Systems, Inc., San Antonio, Texas

 ASSIGNMENT:

Students write short stories using their planning sheets (Student Handout 7) and the directions on the assignment sheet (Student Handout 6). A student/teacher conference may be held after the students complete the planning sheets, to discuss story ideas and problems or questions. The teacher should check regularly on the students' progress.

EXTENSION:

Students may wish to try writing various types of short stories. Refer to Student Handouts 10 (p. 67), and 11 (p. 68), "Adventure Story" and "Science Fiction Story." Distribute these handouts to students who wish to continue exploring short story writing.

CHILDREN'S STORY

 **OBJECTIVE:**

To write an original children's story

FOCUS ACTIVITY:

Ask students to recall a favorite children's story. Share brief synopses of these stories and have individuals discuss why they think particular stories became memorable. Point out elements such as fantasy, suspense, realism, the "happily ever after" ending, etc.

PROCESS:

The teacher or a student reads one or two children's stories to the class. Students discuss interest level, literary elements, and illustrations. The teacher should also contrast an excellent children's book with a poor or mediocre book. The class should discuss what makes a book interesting and eye-catching for children. Have available a variety of books for different age levels as well as examples of fantasy and realistic fiction. Point out the differences in books for preschool through grade five. Give students time to examine and read several books. Their analysis should include setting, plot development, characterization, vocabulary (appropriate level), and artistic appeal.

ASSIGNMENT:

Students write and illustrate their own children's stories. Students may work with a partner or alone. Students choose the age or grade level, type of fiction (realistic or fantasy), and type and number of illustrations (freehand, computer graphics, etc.). The students should have several days to work on this assignment in class. When the stories are completed, the teacher should ask permission for the students to visit an elementary school and read their stories to three or four classes.

EXTENSION:

Students complete one or both of the following activities.

1.   Students work with the art department to illustrate their stories.

2.   Students submit their story manuscripts to children's book publishers.
      See Student Handout 12 (p. 69), "Publishers of Children's Books."

OBJECTIVE:

To write a series of formula poems and a variety of free verse or rhyming poems
To demonstrate an understanding of literary devices such as simile, metaphor, personification, and allusion
To develop an illustrated poetry notebook

FOCUS ACTIVITY:

Read several poems aloud. Have students share their immediate reactions. Discuss the forms and subjects of the poems. Stress that poetry is the written development of a thought or an emotion.

PROCESS:

1. Distribute copies of several poems. Read some of the poems aloud, some silently. Discuss and analyze the poems for content, emotional impact, literary devices, visual imagery, tone, and mood. Discuss differences between poetry and prose.

2. Model formula poems. Distribute Student Handout 13 (pp. 70-79), "Poetry Forms." Discuss examples of the formula poems. Also discuss the development of free verse and rhyming poetry.

©ECS Learning Systems, Inc., San Antonio, Texas

ASSIGNMENT:

Distribute Student Handout 14 (pp. 80-83), "Poetry Notebook." By following the instructions on the handout, each student develops an illustrated poetry notebook. Most of the work for the assignment, with the exception of the illustrations, is done in class. This gives the teacher time to spend with each student, discussing the development of the student's poetry.

Note: Examples for part II, E and part II, G are found in the Student Work section, pp. 91-92.

STUDENT HANDOUTS

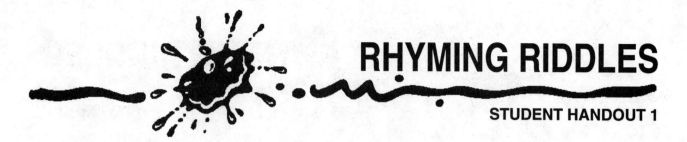

RHYMING RIDDLES

Think of a descriptive name for each of the following phrases. The name must be composed of two rhyming words. Examples:

>second of three puzzles—middle riddle
>implement for watering a plant—rose hose

- very good evergreen
- iron cauldron
- large rodent's high temperature
- foul smell of a small river
- abducted punctuation mark
- tenting place for hoboes
- sole male offspring
- meager flower
- truly good bargain
- mob chattering
- royal bird
- explorer's negative thoughts
- old story
- costless woody plant
- lunar song
- humble Arab ruler
- battle of revenge
- very warm kettle
- fee for medicine
- wooden nickel
- less strong talker
- healthier watcher of children
- whiter mariner
- doleful father
- proud monster
- foolish flower
- nice forest
- ultraviolet shelter for animals
- curious flower
- good for nothing flower
- second of three stringed instruments
- tall clouds
- a very warm place
- timid male
- cold chair
- scarlet hair
- angry seed

©ECS Learning Systems, Inc., San Antonio, Texas

RHYMING RIDDLES

ANSWER KEY FOR STUDENT HANDOUT 1

fine pine
metal kettle
beaver's fever
creek reek
stolen colon
tramp camp
one son
few rue
real steal
loud crowd
regal eagle
scout's doubts
stale tale
free tree
moon tune
meek sheik
mean scene
hot pot
pill bill
plug slug
weaker speaker
fitter sitter
paler sailor
sad dad
braggin' dragon
silly lily
kind pine
black shack
nosy posy
lazy daisy
middle fiddle
high sky
hot spot
coy boy
cool stool
red head
mean bean

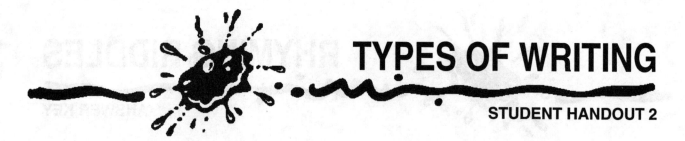

TYPES OF WRITING

DESCRIPTIVE WRITING

When an author wishes to create a mental picture of a subject, (s)he uses descriptive detail. This picture may be of a person, place, thing, event, or experience. The author may report what (s)he sees accurately and objectively, or (s)he may interpret what is seen with a slant toward an impression (s)he wishes to create for the reader. Description is often only a part of a longer piece of writing. An author may devote a phrase, a sentence, a paragraph, or several paragraphs to allowing the reader to see, hear, feel, taste, and/or smell what the author is describing.

NARRATIVE WRITING

Narrative writing is an account of a series of events, usually arranged in chronological order. This account may be real or imaginary and may range from a simple narration of one event to the plot development of an entire novel. The events of a narrative should follow a definite pattern and should be unified by the characterization, setting, and theme. The author should include descriptive detail and explanatory material. The flashback device can also be effective in narrative writing.

EXPOSITORY WRITING

In expository writing, the author gives information or explains facts and ideas. The writer appeals directly to the reader's understanding and explains how to do something, what something means, why it is important, how it works, and/or when and where it occurs.

PERSUASIVE WRITING

In persuasive writing, the author attempts to persuade the reader. Editorials are excellent examples of persuasive writing. To write a good persuasive paper, the author must be able to see both sides of an issue, thus countering any anticipated objections. An author of a good persuasive paper gives several points that support his/her position. Advertising and propaganda are other examples of persuasive writing.

NARRATIVE WRITING

PERSONAL EXPERIENCE

Read the following narrative. It was written as a notebook entry in 1856 by Nathaniel Hawthorne after he had visited the West Derby Workhouse.

After this, we went to the ward where the children were kept; and on entering this, we saw, in the first place, two or three very unlovely and unwholesome little imps, who were lazily playing together. One of them (a child about six years old, but I know not whether a girl or boy) immediately took the strangest fancy to me; it was a wretched, pale, half-torpid little thing, with a humor in its eyes, which the Governor said was the scurvy. I never saw (till a few moments afterwards) a child that I should feel less inclined to fondle. But this little sickly, humor-eaten fright prowled around me, taking hold of my skirts, following at my heels; and at last held up its hands, smiled in my face, and standing directly before me, insisted on my taking it up! Not that it said a word (for I rather think the imp was underwitted, and could not talk) but its face expressed such perfect confidence that it was going to be taken up and made much of, that it was impossible not to do it. It was as if God had promised the child this favor on my behalf, (but I wished He had not!) and that I must needs fulfil the contract. I held my undesirable burthen a little while; and after setting the child down, it still followed me, holding two of my fingers (luckily the glove was on) and playing with them just as if (God save us!) it were a child of my own. It was a foundling; and out of all human kind, it chose me to be its father! We went up stairs into another ward; and on coming down again, there was this same child, waiting for me, with a sickly smile around its scabby mouth and in its dim, red eyes. If it were within the limit of possibility—if I had ever done such wickedness as could have produced this child—I should certainly have set down its affection to the score of blood-recognition; and I cannot conceive of any greater remorse than a parent must feel, if he could see such a result of his illegitimate embraces. I wish I had not touched the imp; and yet I never should have forgiven myself if I had repelled its advances.

ASSIGNMENT:

After reading the narrative and discussing the feelings it produces, write about a similar situation from your own experiences. Choose a time when you felt uncomfortable or when you encountered an unpleasant situation. Perhaps you found it necessary or advisable to react in a way contrary to your personal feelings.

PERSONALITY T-SHIRT

Design a T-shirt JUST FOR YOU. Let it express your personality, your goals, etc. State three reasons why you designed the shirt the way you did.

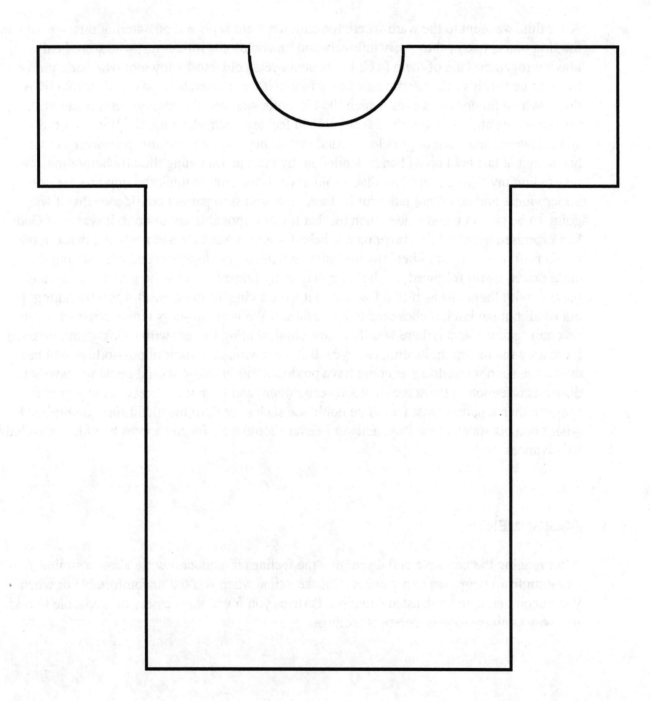

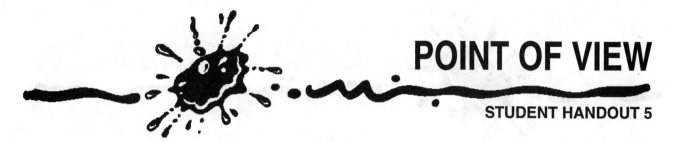

THE THREE LITTLE PIGS—REVISED
by Christy Mata

I'm sure you've heard the story of the three sweet, innocent, little pigs. Sweet, my foot! To this day, I don't understand what happened. All I know is that I lost not only my job, but my dignity as well.

It all began one beautiful spring morning. I was sitting in my office, filing my nails, when I received three "request to build" slips. Now I, as you probably don't know, was the assistant manager of Elmo's Building Inspectors. My job as inspector of new buildings was one of many tedious duties. Not only did I have to grant building permits, but I also had to make sure the coffee pot was always full, and finally, I had to inspect all new buildings. Yes, I was a wolf of many talents—until those little pigs came into town.

Those pigs each filed a request for a building permit for a new home. I, being the kind-hearted wolf that I am, granted their requests. Everything was great until three months later.

I had just filled the coffee pot when Elmo, my boss, called and instructed me to go inspect three new buildings. I prepared my super-deluxe inspection kit and proceeded to leave for work. On my way to the inspection site, I began to think about my past inspections. I had gotten a few complaints insinuating that they were not thorough enough. I came to the conclusion that I must make them more efficient, and today I intended to institute new methods of inspection. After all, I did want to keep my job!

An idea hit me just as I arrived at the first inspection site. If a building could survive a tornado, well, it could survive anything! I knocked on the door, and in my friendliest voice asked the occupant to let me in. I heard somebody say something about a "chin," so, thinking I had been misunderstood, I knocked again and received the same reply. Kids! I asked myself how a tornado would act in this situation. Immediately, I had my answer; with my reputation as a hot-winded wolf, I also had the necessary equipment.

I called out, "I'll huff and I'll puff, and I'll blow your house down!" Now, I didn't mean it literally, but all of a sudden—WHOOOOSH! Oh, no…I couldn't believe it, but I had blown the house down. All that was left was a big mess of straw.

Oh well, if a house couldn't take a little puff of air then it certainly couldn't pass the building inspection. I left my card, with a note explaining the situation, on the doorstep, uh…what had been the doorstep. I felt bad about the house, but life goes on, and I had other jobs waiting.

I proceeded to the next site, a nice stick house. Hmmm, which method of inspection should I use now? I decided that I might as well use the Ol' Huff and Puff test. After all, I was a professional building inspector, and this test would show the true colors of the house's strength.

The occupant and I went through the same old routine that I had experienced at the previous house, only this time, two voices seemed to be saying "chin." I just replied, "I'll huff and I'll puff, and I'll blow your house down!"

WHOOOOSH!

Oops, not again. Once a beautiful house; now a big mess of firewood. What in the world was I to do? I looked everywhere for the owner of the place, but I just couldn't find him. You'd think the owner would stick around and let me explain. Again, I left my card on the doorstep area.

Inspection site number three was a beautiful brick house. I was about to begin the Huff and Puff test when I began thinking that maybe this test was too strict. Nah, it was a test of truth; actually, I was rather enjoying myself anyway.

I knocked on the door and heard nothing. I know the pigs claimed to have said something, but that's their version of the story. It's not my fault that their story is wrong. Since I did not receive an answer, I began my Huff and Puff test.

"I'll huff and I'll puff, and I'll blow your house down!" Man, I tried that test three times, and nothing happened. I just couldn't believe my eyes—the house had survived! Since no one would let me in, I climbed up on the house and peered down the chimney; well, actually, I lost my balance and fell in, and the last thing I remember was being doused with hot water!

Honestly, it took weeks for me to recover from those burns; in fact, I still have some scars. I swear to you that I didn't chase, threaten, or even try to scare those stupid little pigs. I was just a building inspector trying to do an honest job for an honest living. The next thing I knew, however, I had received a notice of a lawsuit, and I had lost my job.

Well, folks, that's my story. I only want to proclaim my innocence, regain my dignity, and get my old job back. Whether you believe me or not, this is the truth, the whole truth, and nothing but the truth…more or less.

 ©ECS Learning Systems, Inc., San Antonio, Texas

SHORT STORY

SHORT STORY ASSIGNMENT:

As you go through the following steps, fill out the planning sheet (Student Handout 8). Create your story. It can be about any subject. It can be insightful, adventurous, or mysterious. Make the unreal seem real—that's what fiction writing is all about.

DIRECTIONS:

1.   Choose characters (protagonist and antagonist).

   Protagonist: the main character—a leading figure in terms of his/her ability to enlist the interest and sympathy of the reader

   Antagonist: the character who stands directly opposed to the protagonist

2.   Choose point of view (first person, third person limited, third person omniscient, etc.).

3.   Choose setting.

4.   Decide on elements of conflict.

5.   Identify sequence of events (plot).

6.   Remember:

   A.   Dialogue can be an effective way of revealing character.

   B.   Set the mood quickly.

   C.   Foreshadowing is an excellent technique.

   D.   Conflict can be external (protagonist vs. another character or natural force) or internal (protagonist's struggle with his/her faults or ideals).

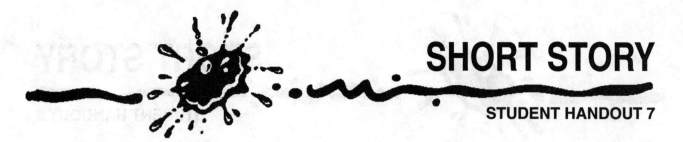

SHORT STORY

PLANNING SHEET

What :
I am writing a story about _____

_____

Materials:

| Characters | Setting |
Protagonist, Antagonist, Others	Time, Place, Mood
_____	_____
_____	_____
_____	_____
_____	_____
_____	_____

Steps:
Sequence of Events_____

_____

_____

_____

_____

_____

_____

©ECS Learning Systems, Inc., San Antonio, Texas

Conflict:
Problem situations in the story. Be sure to list the characters who are involved in the conflict.

_____

_____

_____

_____

_____

_____

_____

_____

Problems in Putting the Story Together:

_____

_____

_____

_____

_____

_____

STRUCTURE AND ELEMENTS OF PLOT

The plot is the sequence of events in the story.

The five parts of plot structure:

A. **Exposition**: an introduction to the main characters, settings, and situations of the story

B. **Rising Action**: the events and complications that lead to an important dramatic point in the story

C. **Climax**: the point of greatest interest and emotional involvement in the story; turning point of the story

D. **Falling Action**: the events that develop from the climax and lead to the conclusion

E. **Denouement**: the final outcome of the story; also called the resolution

Every short story has a plot, which gives the story its basic shape or form. It tells the reader "what happens" in a story.

Plot Development

I. Conflict

Conflict, the struggle between two opposing forces, is the heart of the plot. It can be external conflict or internal conflict.

A. **External conflict**: protagonist struggles against an outside force such as another person, society, nature, or fate.

B. **Internal conflict**: struggle occurs within the protagonist. For example, (s)he may struggle to reach an important decision or to make a difficult moral choice.

 ©ECS Learning Systems, Inc., San Antonio, Texas

II. Ways to Develop the Plot

    A. Suspense

    B. Foreshadowing

    C. Flashback

    D. Surprise ending

III. Characterization

    A. Direct—making direct statements about the character

    B. Indirect—revealing the character through events in the story (his/her actions or dialogue)

IV. Setting

Setting establishes the time and place of action in a story.

STORY STARTERS

A piercing scream broke the stillness of the night…

The ambulance screamed into the night…

The blizzard raged around our stalled car…

Miles and miles of burning desert stretched ahead…

He only remembered leaving the party and getting into his car…

Fear engulfed me with every step…

I couldn't believe my eyes…

All the students in school waited anxiously…

We'd searched every section of the campground…

Memories filled my mind as my parents announced their separation…

The note under the pillow stated…

Every step brought me closer to my dream…

I stared at my dad through the thick, ugly bars as I tried to remember why I was here…

The weathered house, the only home John had ever known, was gone…

The lovely little cottage had become a menacing trap…

It was just an "innocent" prank, but the lights from police cars were flashing everywhere…

ADVENTURE STORY

Adventure stories are filled with danger, excitement, and challenges. Because they are about people who challenge life, and because our lives are made up of large and small challenges, these tales never go out of style. Adventure stories tell about people who dare, who take risks, and who explore the unknown. The word **adventure** is derived from a Latin root which means "to arrive" or "to come to." The protagonist in an adventure story usually "arrives" at the end of the quest. The adventure has changed the protagonist physically and mentally, and (s)he has become stronger and wiser. The adventurer has wrestled with, and usually conquered, a challenge. Life will never again be the same.

Classic pattern for an adventure story:

A. The hero or heroine encounters some opposing force. This may be an element of society, the forces of nature, another person, or combination of these.

B. In the struggle, the hero or heroine must eventually endure some type of "trial for life."

C. The hero or heroine is changed by the adventure; (s)he becomes wiser, stronger, or more capable of handling life. The adventurer may also cause a change in the world.

SHORT STORY

SCIENCE FICTION STORY

Create an imaginary world as the setting, invent characters for that world, and develop a plot involving the characters. Remember, all the basics of good story writing apply here as well.

Ideas for a science fiction story:

I. Setting of the New World

   A. Name of the planet
   B. The planet's historical background
   C. Types of transportation found on this planet
   D. Religious structure of the new world
   E. Government in the new world

II. Characters

   A. Appearance
   B. Longevity
   C. Family structure
   D. Dominant physical traits
   E. Dominant mental traits

III. Plot and Theme Development

   A. Invasion by aliens
   B. Political upheaval/government coup
   C. Travel outside the planet for the first time
   D. Population explosion

©ECS Learning Systems, Inc., San Antonio, Texas

PUBLISHERS OF CHILDREN'S BOOKS

The following is a partial list of publishers of children's literature. If you are interested in submitting any of your stories for possible publication, write for specifications. Be sure to enclose a self-addressed, stamped envelope.

Abingdon Press
201 Eighth Ave., S.
Nashville, TN 37202

Adama Books
306 W. 38th St.
New York, NY 10018

Bantam Books
666 Fifth Ave.
New York, NY 10103

Barron's
113 Crossways Park Dr.
Woodbury, NY 11797

Bradbury Press
866 Third Ave.
New York, NY 10022

Carolrhoda Books
241 First Ave., N.
Minneapolis, MN 55401

Clarion Books
Ticknor & Fields
52 Vanderbilt Ave.
New York, NY 10017

Crown Publishers
225 Park Ave., S.
New York, NY 10017

Dodd, Mead & Co.
71 Fifth Ave.
New York, NY 10003

Farrar, Strauss & Giroux
19 Union Sq. W.
New York, NY 10003

Harper and Row
10 E. 53rd St.
New York, NY 10022

Houghton Mifflin
2 Park St.
Boston, MA 02108

Joy Street Books
Little, Brown
34 Beacon St.
Boston, MA 02108

Alfred A. Knopf
201 E. 50th St.
New York, NY 10022

Philomel Books
Putnam Publishing
51 Madison Ave.
New York, NY 10010

Charles Scribner's Sons
Macmillan Publishing
866 Third Ave.
New York, NY 10022

Viking Penguin
40 W. 23rd St.
New York, NY 10010

Franklin Watts
387 Park Ave., S.
New York, NY 10016

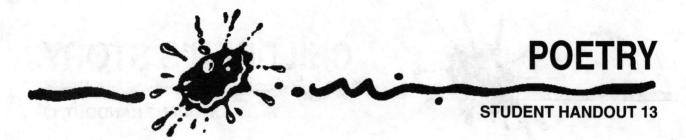

Poetry Forms

Haiku

The haiku is a Japanese poem in three lines of 5, 7, and 5 syllables. It may be sad or gay, deep or frivolous, religious, humorous, or satirical. It is designed to give an image that is a starting point for thought and emotion. The rules which govern the syllables do not have to be strictly followed; syllables can vary one or two per line.

Autumn leaves piled high
small feet take a running start
Whoosh! gold leaves scatter

Cinquain

The cinquain is similar to the haiku; it consists of five lines.

Line 1: one word (noun) to give the title

Line 2: two words to describe the title

Line 3: three words to express action concerning the title

Line 4: four words to express feeling about the title

Line 5: one word that is a synonym for the title

Sunrise
Pink, orange
Rising, coloring, warming
The silent sky awakes
Dawn

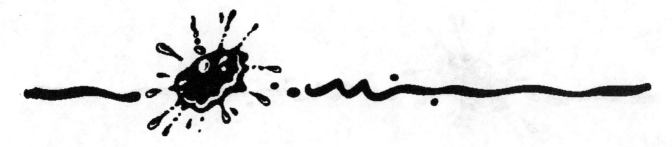

Diamente

The diamente is a seven-line contrast poem that is set up to appear in a diamond shape on paper.

Line 1: one word (a noun, the subject)

Line 2: two words (adjectives describing line 1)

Line 3: three words ("ing" or "ed" words that relate to line 1)

Line 4: four words (first two nouns relate to line 1; second two nouns to line 7)

Line 5: three words ("ing" or "ed" words that relate to line 7)

Line 6: two words (adjectives describing line 7)

Line 7: one word (noun that is the opposite of line 1)

Contrast in thought occurs in line 4. Most people find it easier to start with lines 1 and 7.

Life
Exuberant, vivacious
Laughing, playing, loving
Brother, birthday, Grandfather, funeral
Crying, suffering, empty
Sorrowful, tragic
Death

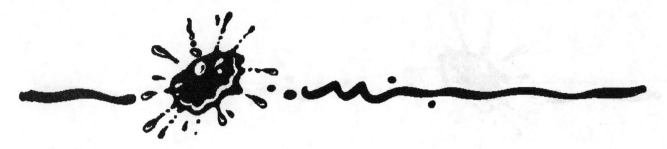

Metaphor/Simile Poem

A **metaphor** is a comparison which does not use "like" or "as" but rather takes the form of a direct statement. (Example: Fear is a bottomless pit.)

A **simile** is a comparison between two things; they are linked with the word "like" or "as." (Example: He was as white as a sheet.)

Metaphor Poem

Line 1: noun

Line 2-4: write something about the subject; each line should say something different and give an idea of what the subject is like.

Line 5: a metaphor that begins with the title

> Fear
> Apprehensive about the future
> Afraid hidden faults will be revealed
> Uncertainty looms on every side
> Fear is a bottomless pit.

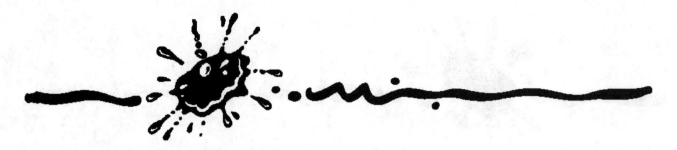

Lanterne

The Japanese have several forms of poetry based on the arrangement of syllables. One of these forms has a pattern of 1-2-3-4-1 syllables arranged in the shape of a Japanese lantern; therefore, it is called the lanterne. It is possible to join several verses together in the form of a linked or chained lanterne, also. This practice creates a more complete story.

The Start of Life

The
Very
Inception
Of life begins
Fast

The
Egg grows
Rapidly
Into a live
Form

A Living
Breathing ball
Of human flesh
Grows

And
Becomes
A child that
Will Become a
Man

Limerick

A limerick is a five-line nonsense poem. The first, second, and fifth lines rhyme and have three stresses. The third and fourth lines rhyme and have two stresses. This verse form allows you to let your imagination run wild, even to the point of making up your own words!

There once was a toe name of Lou
Who frequently cried out "Boo Hoo!"
With each day that passed,
He was constantly smashed.
But so were the other nine, too!

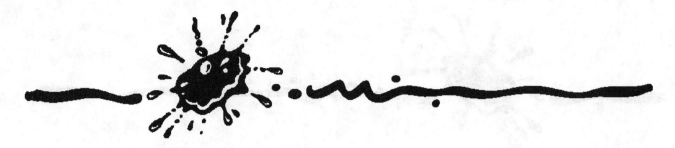

Shaped Whimsey

One of the most imaginative forms of poetry is the shaped whimsey. In this form, the story of a poem is printed within a certain shape, which reflects the subject of the poem. A raindrop might contain a poem on the subject of falling rain. The shapes should be simple and to the point.

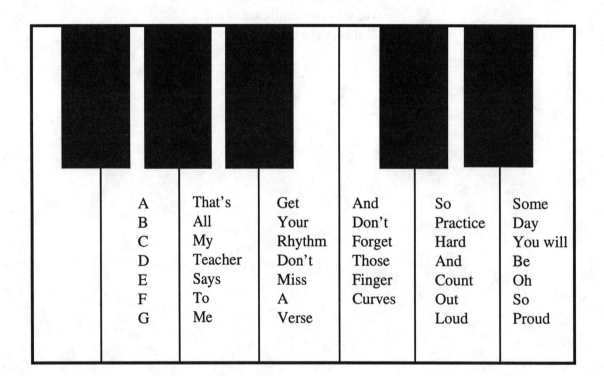

©ECS Learning Systems, Inc., San Antonio, Texas

Part-of-Speech Poem

Line 1: article + noun

Line 2: adjective + conjunction + adjective

Line 3: verb + conjunction + verb

Line 4: adverb

Line 5: noun relating to the noun in the first line

> The wrinkle
> Unannounced, yet definite
> Carves and defines
> Immediately
> Face

Name Poem

Use the letters of a name for the first letter of each line.

KELLY

Kind
Everlasting friendship
Loves to make people laugh
Likes to please everyone
Yields to everyone in need

Five-Senses Poem

This formula poem, which deals with an emotion, is developed by using the five senses. Choose an emotion such as fear, anger, jealousy, love, apprehension, etc., then follow the five steps below.

Line 1: color of the emotion
Line 2: sound of the emotion
Line 3: taste of the emotion
Line 4: smell of the emotion
Line 5: sight (what the emotion looks like)
Line 6: feeling evoked by the emotion

Obsession

Obsession is the color of the fiery sun that torments the Sahara;
It sounds like an angry wind
And tastes like honey-coated sand.
It smells like a smoking gun;
It looks like pyrite.
It makes me feel insatiable.

Obsession is green with greed;
It sounds like hysterical laughter
And tastes like cheap wine.
It smells like a rose that has rotted.
Obsession looks like a rabid dog foaming at the mouth;
It makes me feel crazed.

Obsession is the color of a stormy northern sky;
It sounds like a sax bellowing its mournful tune.
It tastes like bittersweet chocolates
And smells like a man's strong cologne.
It looks like an addict sobbing in a dark alley.
Obsession makes me feel burdened.

Obsession is the fine line that separates
love from hate.

Thanks to the following students for allowing use of their work: Michelle Finney, Amber Green, Jennifer Green, Wendy Green, Ad Godinez, Kimberly Harris, Kevin King, Stacy McElroy, Amy Montgomery, and Lisa Noble.

POETRY NOTEBOOK

Create a poetry notebook. It must contain the following sections. It should be colorful and illustrated.

A.   Fly Sheet

B.   Title Page

      1.   An original name for your notebook
      2.   Your name and class period
      3.   The date

C.   Table of Contents

D.   Specified Exercises

Specified Exercises

Part I

Write an original poem for each of the following types of poetry.

A.   Haiku
B.   Cinquain
C.   Diamente
D.   Metaphor/Simile poem
E.   Lanterne
F.   Limerick
G.   Shaped whimsey
H.   Part-of-speech poem
I.   Name poem
J.   Five-senses poem

Part II

Complete the following sections.

A.   What was the happiest time in your past? Did you realize at the time how happy you were? If you appreciate this happiness more in retrospect than you did at the time, do you feel regretful, amused, or nostalgic? Considering these questions, write a poem about a happy time in your past.

B.   Write a poem about the last time you saw (choose one):

      1.   A particular person
      2.   A particular place
      3.   A particular object

C.   Write a minimum of three poems based on any of the following "list" ideas.

      1.   **Past Lists**: List your earliest memories, based on these ideas: things you regret having done or not having done; the food and all the surrounding details of memorable meals; friends with whom you have lost contact; all the names you can remember from your first-grade class; all the pets you have ever owned; strange sights you have seen.

      2.   **Future Lists**: List strange, exotic things you want to do; things you want to accomplish in life; things you want to do tomorrow; things you would like to do with someone; things you expect your future to bring.

      3.   **Object Lists**: List things in your favorite room; things in a room you dislike; things in your desk, pockets, or purse; things in someone's attic, storage room, or closet; things you have seen in a pawnshop window or some other sort of business; all the objects you can remember having lost in your lifetime.

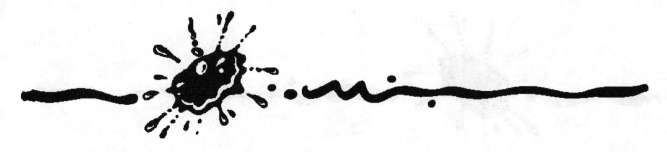

4. **Dream Lists**: List recurring dreams or fantasies.

5. **Favorite Lists**: Make lists of your favorite heroes, possessions, clothes, friends, or places.

6. **Dislike Lists**: Make lists of foods you dislike; bad habits (your own or other people's); boring days or events in your life; chores you dislike; times in history that trouble you.

7. **Word Lists**: Collect words that appeal to you.

D. Write a poem about something very small (atom, drop of water, grain of sand, etc.). Include all of its features, actions, etc. Compare or contrast this object with something very large. Variation: Choose something nearby and relate it to something far away.

E. Write a "string" poem about any subject you choose. A string poem can be about any subject, but it will always have a twist at the end.

F. Choose one of the following:

1. Write a poem addressed to another self—your alter ego, or your image in the mirror. Do not explain that you are addressing yourself; let that come out in the poem.

2. Write a poem addressed to an anonymous "You" in which you evoke a particular mood or emotional state with concrete images. Examples: loneliness, anger, guilt, happiness.

G. Write a poem beginning with one of the following lines. Think of some real experience that would fit the line and write your poem to bring out its significance. If you prefer, you can invent something fantastic and dreamlike.

1. That door is closed…

2. I see a stairway leading…

3. A journey lies ahead…

4. I see a face at the window…

5. Something is slipping away…

6. What is happening to me?

7. Help me! I am falling…

8. I enter a room…

9. Something seems familiar…

10. I have been here before…

11. I wish I could remember…

12. Today is just the beginning…

H. Add as many free verse or rhyming poems as you wish. Express yourself, because that is what creative writing is all about.

NOTES

STUDENT WORK

A SPECIAL DAY
by Kendra Wilson

I had anticipated the event for weeks. When the day of the Special Olympics arrived, all my fears surfaced. I knew I couldn't possibly turn back now; I must face my fears. I remember getting on the bus and sitting next to Cari Ann. Cari is very garrulous, and I was interested in trying to fathom the things going through her mind. I knew that many things in my future depended on the emotions I would feel at the upcoming event. I was scared stiff that I wouldn't be brave enough to overcome my fears; therefore, I might destroy my future.

We finally arrived and I felt as though I might "bust" at any given moment. The competitors' enthusiasm was contagious and I was ready for things to get started. As soon as the events got underway, it was amazing to watch the sheer joy and fulfillment that spread across each individual's face. At the 50-meter wheelchair race, I saw a young man, about my age, struggling beyond belief to reach the finish line. Long after everyone else had crossed the line, he was alone, still struggling. The "roar of the crowd" was deafening. I could not stop thinking about all the effort he put into one race. Trying to imagine myself in his place made me realize that I would already have given up. Seeing the unremitting determination in his eyes brought tears to mine. Someone told me that if those were tears of pity that I would be wise to "dry it up." At first I thought this to be a cruel remark, but when I saw the glow of victory on his face, even though he had lost, I realized that I was the handicapped one.

I know that I am not physically or mentally handicapped, but as far as being content or thankful, I know that I am. Watching someone my own age struggle made me realize all the things I take for granted. It occurred to me that it would be an excellent idea to learn from them rather than try to teach them everything about "our" way of thinking. I will admit that I still had a tendency to pity them, thinking how different their lives are from mine.

Cari Ann informed me that I was wrong when she began to discuss boyfriends with me. Later on in our conversation, she told me, "That's what Special Olympics is all about."

"What's that, Cari?" I asked.

She was gripping a green ribbon in her small hand and exclaimed, "Winning fifth place, that's what it is all about!"

I can only pray that someday I can be the kind of person these people are. My hopes and future goals were only confirmed by my special experience at Special Olympics.

The student who wrote this plans to work professionally with handicapped children.

©ECS Learning Systems, Inc., San Antonio, Texas

RECORD-A-DREAM
by Toby Carpenter, Jaime Reyes, Troy Watson, Chris Young

The students who prepared this advertising campaign demonstrated their product with a video presentation in class. It was effective and enjoyable. They introduced it with the following statements:

Record-A-Dream is a "dream" come true. All of your dreams can finally become reality! Have you ever had a dream that you wished you could record? Now you can, with the all-new Record-A-Dream. Yes, it's true! You can actually record your most wonderful, passionate, and scary dreams with this painless method. If you follow the directions correctly, your dreams will come out on a VCR tape, and it will be something for everyone to enjoy. Parents, do you want to know what your children are thinking and dreaming? Now you can with the Record-A-Dream. This machine is safe and can be used by people of all ages. Only $199.00; call 1-800-DREAMER; money-back guarantee.

Promotional Material:

TV commercial (with special TV offer), newspaper, magazine
Designed to appeal to all the senses as a product that is vital to life
Created for anyone who could use the product as a luxury or as a vital piece of equipment
Could be used to study human behavior in the field of psychology

Targeted Market:

- Dreamers who would like to know what they see in their sleep
- Fortune tellers
- Movie enthusiasts
- Parents
- Spouses

Price:

$199.00

Prediction:

This product will develop into a billion-dollar market just as the color TV and VCR market.

CHARACTERIZATION

HANNA

Hanna Renae Watson visited the creative writing class at Muleshoe High School on September 6, 1988. Seventeen students at the junior or senior level observed her for several minutes, then wrote their observations of her looks and her personality. Based on their findings, the students wrote a composite characterization, including a projection of the young lady that Hanna will someday become.

As Hanna proceeded to and fro, she reminded us of a pigeon-toed princess waddling through her kingdom. She stared at us from large, curious eyes that were the color of the sea; she entertained us with a melodic, yet foreign speech. Her tasseled corn-silk hair wispily framed her pixie face. She had a pert nose and protruding ears, and her chin was always wet from her lolling tongue. Her magnificent personality shone the most whenever she smiled a toothy grin.

Hanna, a unique and jubilant child, illustrated her personality by her actions. As she carried herself across the room, we felt as if we were in Hanna's kingdom. She had the signs of an intelligent, mature, and independent little girl. Eager to explore and ready to play, her smile expressed her contentment and her happy behavior. Her smiles seemed to invite a friend; she was curious to know anything and anyone. Babbling along in her "language," it seemed as though she would talk your ear off. Hanna's strong personality sets a good foundation for the rest of her life.

As we looked beyond her personality traits, we decided that she will be several things in future years. Her flamboyant personality, combined with her blond silky hair, illuminating blue eyes, and beautiful pale complexion reveal the probability for future popularity. The early independence she possesses indicates that she is a born leader. This young lady's unique mind will guide her through several indescribable events. Through careful observation, we concluded that the future holds many things for this bright young lady.

Other observations included Hanna's contentment and her attachment to a "security" blanket and her thumb. This precocious little girl was ready to discover new things, and she was not afraid of unfamiliar people or different surroundings. In fact, one student felt that Hanna constantly has a million things going through her mind and would ask numerous questions if she could just talk. It was observed that she very likely keeps her parents on their toes at all times. One student mentioned that Hanna looks like a baby who might appear on a diaper commercial. Today, this adorable, one-year-old baby girl was, indeed, a star!

©ECS Learning Systems, Inc., San Antonio, Texas

THE COACH
by Wade King

Everyone in the gym shared the lump in Coach's throat. He had watched these young men grow, both on the football field and off. Over the past seven years he had shared, and was largely responsible for, some of the greatest accomplishments of their young lives. But now he was helping them through one of their worst experiences.

It was a cool August morning as the fall of 1980 was just beginning. Young boys all over Texas were preparing for the upcoming football season, but this August morning was something more to a certain group of these boys and to their rangy new coach. For the boys, it was the beginning of their schoolboy football era. For Coach, it was the beginning of a new career.

Coach towered above the boys, not as any coach does over his seventh-grade players, but as Goliath over his men. He was huge, all of six feet, four inches, while the tallest boy was approximately five-eight. If a player dared to make a mistake, Coach let him know it. He would pull the shaking boy's face mask within an inch of his face and yell until we expected the boy's helmet to fly off, head and all. Needless to say, the same boy rarely made the same mistake twice.

At the end of the season, Coach went on to high school to become a varsity assistant, while the boys continued their junior high school lives as normal teenage boys would. Something special, however, had been sparked between the coach and his boys.

A few years, a few pounds, and a few inches later, the boys met up with Coach again, this time as junior varsity players on a team for which he was now the coach. The boys had grown, were no longer green, and had even chased a couple of district championships pretty hard. The most noticeable change, however, could be seen in Coach. He was not the same tyrant who had yelled at the boys while they were learning to be football players. He had loosened up and now seemed to be a good friend.

This football season was to be the greatest experience of their short football careers, but as it began, this was hard for them to realize. They lined up in practice day in and day out and let one of the best teams in the state of Texas—their own varsity—batter them with all they had. But Coach made even that seem fun. The season got underway, and as they won a few games under his expert leadership, they realized that they had a special team, with a special coach. Through his leadership and the players' willingness to work for him, they brought a district championship home to Muleshoe, and it seemed the winning would only continue during the next two years.

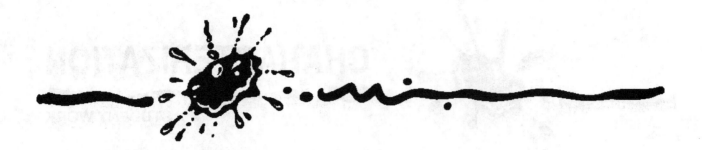

This did not turn out to be true the next year, however, as they experienced a losing season. But, as only he could do, Coach held together the boys who were left, and through his willingness to talk and listen, he kept the spark of hope alive in the young men.

When those young men came to start their last season as high school football players, Coach was there to meet them. He was the same joker who seemed like a friend, but with a different twist; this was varsity high school football and it was time to get serious. The odds were against these young men, but they knew they could win with a little hard work; when the cards were dealt, however, it was not so easy. The community supported them as much as a small Texas town can support a zero and nine team. But that just was not enough for a group of young men who had dreamed of their chance to play Texas schoolboy football and to win. There was one thing, however, that pulled them through this very difficult time, and that was the support of their friend and mentor.

Now, as they prepared for the last football game they would ever play, at the end of a season without a win, the young men remembered the man who had always been there for them in good times as well as bad. The last thing a football team should have been thinking about at a time like this was their coach, but this group of players had a special advisor and friend. It was time, at the last pep rally of the season, to honor Coach, and they did. As he struggled for the first words to say on this occasion, the crowd could feel the bond between this coach and his men.

Through these six years, the bond between the men and their coach had only grown. This was not merely a one-way closeness; the members of the football team experienced the same closeness for Coach that he felt for them. The men had learned more than how to play a game for the coach; through his leadership, they had developed character. The friendship that had developed and the lessons that had been learned from Coach would follow the men into their adult lives.

This piece was written as a tribute to Jerry Robinson, who now lives in Canyon, Texas.

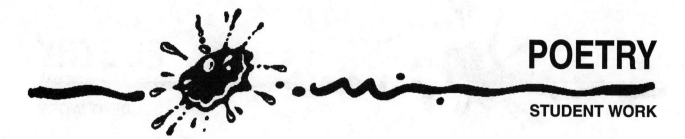
STRING POEMS

I walked into the room
and proudly set the
paper on her desk,
remembering the two weeks
when I had spent every afternoon
straining to make this paper
THE BEST.
"My paper will be perfect!"
I thought.
I asked when the grades
would be announced...
FOR PRACTICE?

by Casey King

That's it!
Who needs him?
He has been nothing but trouble.
Besides, I could do better.
It will be beneficial
For both of us.
I never really liked him;
He is just not good enough for me.
The next time I see him,
I will be sick.

Hello?
OH, HI! YEAH, I MISS YOU, TOO!

by Stacy McElroy

I HAVE BEEN HERE BEFORE
by Caryn Durben

I have been here before!
I recognize that cloud.
You see that bird? He talks to you,
But the only word he knows is "Who."
Be quiet and listen and you will see
That **I** have been here before.

I **have** been here before!
I recognize that tree.
You see those lines carved in that bark?
We did that one night after dark.
It says "Jane loves Johnny and Johnny loves Jane."
I **have** been here before.

I have **been** here before!
I recognize that rose.
This is the only place, you see,
Where roses grow on nettle trees.
Take a deep breath and smell the breeze.
I have **been** here before.

I have been **here** before!
I recognize this place.
You see the smile that's on my face?
It always comes when I'm in this place.
I feel I'm basking in His grace.
I have been **here** before.

I have been here **before**!
This is the first time since,
But I'll be back time and again.
I don't know how; I don't know when.
But I hope I come again and again
To this place I've been to **before**.

 ©ECS Learning Systems, Inc., San Antonio, Texas

NOTES

NOTES

ABOUT THE AUTHOR

PAT WATSON

Patricia (Pat) Ann Watson earned a Bachelor of Music Education degree from Eastern New Mexico University and acquired graduate hours and further certification at Texas Tech University. During her 21 years of teaching, Pat worked at the elementary, junior high, and high school levels. For 10 years, she taught English III, creative writing, and literary genres at Muleshoe High School in Muleshoe, Texas. She was named Muleshoe ISD Teacher of the Year in May, 1993, and Region XVII Secondary Teacher of the Year in August, 1993. Although she retired from classroom teaching in 1994, she continues to present workshops for teachers and to produce teaching material for publication.

Pat has been married to W. T. Watson for 43 years. They have three sons (David, Ed, and Cliff) and 11 grandchildren.